ANONYYMI

A JOY PLAYBOOK

First published by Lillymor 2022

First edition

This book was professionally typeset on Reedsy.
Find out more at reedsy.com

for the matriline

Contents

Foreword

"There is a vitality, a life force, an energy, a quickening that is translated through you into action, and because there is only one of you in all of time, this expression is unique. And if you block it, it will never exist through any other medium and it will be lost. The world will not have it. It is not your business to determine how good it is nor how valuable nor how it compares with other expressions. It is your business to keep it yours clearly and directly, to keep the channel open. You do not even have to believe in yourself or your work. You have to keep yourself open and aware of the urges that motivate you. Keep the channel open. ... No artist is pleased. [There is] no satisfaction whatsoever at any time. There is only a queer divine dissatisfaction, a blessed unrest that keeps us marching and makes us more alive than the others"

— Martha Graham

Preface

I started out with one mission: I accepted a challenge to write and publish this book in seven days.

On Day One, I set up the accounts needed to physically publish my finished book: Reedsy, Canva and KDP (Amazon's self-publishing portal). On Day Two, I had to pick a topic. The prompt was to write down a list of things I always love to talk about, think about, spend time doing etc... I had a pretty big list, but I thought since I know the most about acting and supporting actors to build a career, I thought it would be best to write a book about acting and came up with "The A*List Playbook", a step-by-step career guide for those actors who want to get to their next career level.

The A*List is a fairly insane aspiration for anyone, considering there are eight billion people on the planet and about two hundred A-List actors that actually fall into the "my starring in this film gets it financed" category. But hey! I love outrageous goals. I wouldn't be surprised if there were millions of people who THINK they want to be an A-Lister, but in reality are highly unlikely to ever find themselves green lighting a four-figure film budget, much less an eight or nine-figure movie.

But, anyone who is serious about their acting career could have read that book, taken ALL the actions I'd laid out for them and then who knows? One or two might have actually beaten the one-in-eighty-million odds someday. Either way, they would have at least become a self-supporting working actor with a fan base of some sort.

There is a belief that being a working actor is this impossible thing. In reality, most of the people who "pursue acting", do not take the actions they need to take in order to have a bona fide career. They will say the reason they are not booking the 'next level' job is because of their looks, their age, some reason why the Hollywood system is against them personally, etc... This is just not true.

Basically,

IF YOU ARE:

(1) willing to be honest with yourself and *embrace* where you are, how you present yourself to the world and what you resonate when other people interact with you

(2) invest in quality [advice for] and [creators of] your marketing materials that obviously reflect this embrace as these are the jobs you will actually book (initially) to get your career launched

(3) you behave professionally with everyone connected to the industry

(4) you take daily, strategic actions to audition

AND

(5) you find a teacher who has a significant track record of students who are already working at the next level of your resume and work your tail off in their class until you have the career you aspire to have?

THEN,

YOU WILL BE A WORKING ACTOR, with a five to eight figure income.

It's truly not rocket science.

But like most things we tell ourselves about why we can't have or be or do what we say we really want; the truth is usually that we are unwilling to make the decision to prioritize the aspiration and do the things required to change ourselves and our circumstances because these new actions by their very nature will feel awkward and uncomfortable, at best. The rather tragic irony is that we aspire to comfort at the cost of our true joy. And what other purpose do we really have on this planet other than the pursuit of happiness?

So back to this book. I arrived at Day Four and Five, where I was tasked with writing the content. I found myself going through 'change discomfort'; feeling itchy, spinning, wasting time, being indecisive, doubting everything I'd written and finally hating the fact that I picked this topic, knowing that the idea of pursuing 'An A-List Career' is folly, unless you happen to be one of the twelve hundred people in the group that that is your next logical career step. But it's not just about the crazy odds. It goes deeper.

An actor who makes it to this tiny circle today is most likely a risk taker and a rule breaker, unwilling to trust some other person's idea, if it conflicts with what drives the actor from within. It's this need to work from what is their own authentic impulse that makes their work so alive, unexpected, charismatic and bankable. We all feel a primal truth when we watch them lighting up the screen like heroines. A truth we are all, on some level, starving to experience: the desire to have enough courage to live our own truth, which we know on a soul level is the only thing that matters.

Giving away the infinite power we all possess, the power to define our own A*List is the very reason we are not living our own A*List life. We all have ruby slippers. The Wizard of Oz is still in the mix more than a century after L. Frank Baum's book came out in 1900, because it resonates with a universal human truth in all of us. These ah-ha moments that came out of my chaos and discomfort became my anchor. THIS is what this book wants to be. This is where my pleasure/challenge/meaning collision happens today.

Then, like the miracle that putting our attention on something is, the spiritual power of synchronicity throws me some new bones. An old friend of mine (who I met as a freshman on my first day of architecture school in our Basic Design One class) sent me a text about an article in Dwell magazine featuring a visionary from Philly: the design-obsessed Shannon Maldonado and her hometown storefront, Yowie.

She's pictured interviewing another inspiring creative, Lindsey Scannapieco, who founded the socially progressive architecture design company, Scout. That led me to watch Shannon's you tube pilot for 'Small Enough' where I sat glued to my laptop, listening to her talk about ideas and process, then her fantastic interview with Lindsey. My mind was exploding. Her thoughts resonated so deeply, I felt incredible joy that she exists and lives in the world the way that she does. Listening to her, I felt more courageous to make this imperfect book. To just begin. To allow an unfolding of ideas as they come. To be where I am, so I might go where I belong and in my efforts, hold the hope that I might bring more voices into a new dialogue; yet, at the very same time, accept that it is enough for now to know that I have at least engaged in a new dialogue within myself.

Every fiber of my being was screaming YEEEEEEEESSSSSSSS!!! THIS is what matters. I thought to myself, do I need to move to Philly to be a part of this community? Actually, no. I do not. I already am a part of this community, even if they don't know me. And even if they did know me, they might not feel I am in their tribe. Jack Nicholson does not know I am in his tribe, but I know I am in his tribe. We all belong in the tribe of our role models. We are drawn to them because they are us.

All to say, the only thing for me to do is express what I am, wherever I am, as truly as I am able in each moment. Which sounds so simple. Babies do it. But it's been a very upstream swimming experience ever since I started talking. It has taken me decades to arrive back at this basic level of freedom and truth with which we all come into this life expressing. Some people might say that the modern world is designed to obstruct the process of living an authentic life, but I tend to feel it is the process of overcoming obstacles that strengthen our courage and clarifies our path. A chicken/egg thing.

This book is my love letter to acting and to life, my own chicken/egg thing. I hope it leads to something that sparks you.

INVITATION

This book is your place to play.

The first chapter begins with a look at a relatively recent development in how we as humans approach happiness. There has been a shift in scientific research over the past decade, within the mental health community. A shift in their traditional focus how to improve on what is wrong with humans and all our psychological/emotional maladies, towards researchers using the scientific method, pursuing answers to the question: "What gives people the feeling that life is worth living and how can that feeling be expanded?"

The body of the book is an experiment. Here I've given each page a word, or questions or some ideas or maybe an experience to try, followed by blank space for you to respond, or not, in any way you wish.

And near the end, you will encounter a brief conclusion.

QUEST

For decades scientists have been measuring depression, but concluded that happiness, our universally sought after state of being, was impossible to measure. In 2011, a new documentary came out to challenge that assumption. It's a feature length film called "Happy"; written, directed and co-produced by Academy Award nominated director, Roco Belic.

The film opens with this quote:

> *"The constitution only guarantees the American people the right to pursue happiness. You have to catch it yourself."*
> *–Ben Franklin*

The story it weaves takes us on a compelling journey to fourteen different countries around the world, including interviews with people from a wide spectrum of cultures, economic states, and personal circumstances. The project's sole purpose is to scientifically measure happiness.

Around the world, in all fourteen countries when asked what people wanted most in life, everyone said the same thing: "Happiness." What the filmmaker discovered was that once a person had a modest (but truly livable) income, greater wealth did not increase their happiness. Status of any kind did not increase happiness.

What made the greatest difference to happiness (after acquiring a sustainable income) was a sense of belonging to a community that valued them and spending time with those people doing everyday things like laughing, sharing stories, singing, dancing, or preparing and eating food together.

There were many other activities that individuals consciously choose to do, like performing acts of kindness, a weekly practice of naming five things you are grateful for and any activity that focused on caring about something greater than yourself or the well-being of others that gave people the most substantial happiness. One scientist shared how anyone could fast-track the benefits of meditating with a practice of 'compassion meditation' where after only two weeks of daily practice, people experienced positive changes measured in their brain scans that usually take a meditator years to accomplish.

Overall, they concluded that what makes people happy is different for everyone, but the basic building blocks of happiness stem from doing what you love, playing, having new experiences, spending time with friends, and with family, doing things that are meaningful, and appreciating what we have. These are all things that any of us can choose to do that will increase our happiness. All of these activities are free!

According to Psychologist Martin Seligmann (past president of the American Psychological Association and known as the father of Positive Psychology), there are three ways humans experience happiness.

The first is pleasure, which is derived from having an easy, pleasant life. This type of happiness has a half-life of diminishing returns until no happiness is derived, unless it is paired with challenge and/or meaning.

The second way we experience happiness is with challenge. This is being in the flow state of some activity that captivates your attention in a thrilling way while time flies by without your awareness.

The third form of happiness comes from meaningful experiences. These are characterized by a mission or doing something of service for others and investing time in activities that serve something greater than ourselves.

The research revealed that both meaning and challenge alone or in combination with a second type of happiness, can create lasting fulfillment, but it is only the combination of all three of these types of happiness that generates pure, lasting joy:

PLEASURE + CHALLENGE + MEANING = JOY

This rang true for me. Does it ring true for you? How do you find and express joy? On the following pages I have created an experiment. I have put words or sentences or questions or invitations for you to play with and space for you to respond, as you wish.

DREAM

Many of us have a dream. For some it is so atrophied, it has drifted into the land of their unconscious. For others, it is a regret. Still others have it smoldering. Is it ever too late for a dream? Do you have a dream?

CURIOSITY

Make a list of anything you might be interested in or curious about.

PRACTICE

Decide when you can commit at least 5 minutes each day to some process that you are curious about, one day at a time. Pick a time. Put an alarm in your phone to remind you. Give the alarm its own ringtone. You may only go for those 5 minutes or you may go for 50 minutes or 5 hours, the most important thing is committing to consistency. And all you are committing to is 5 minutes a day. Everything after that is optional.

PASSION

What is the thing you spend the most time thinking about, talking about, reading about, watching others do. Be as specific and as honest as you can be.

ADMIRATION

Whose life do you wish you had? Who do you wish you were more like? Who are your role models?

PLEASURE

What have been the most enjoyable days of your life?

ACTIVITY

What do you love to do? What are you doing when time flies by? What are your hobbies? What do you spend most of your free time doing? Is that activity fun? What would you be doing if you only did what you wanted to do all day?

ASPIRATION

Write down what you dream about most, for your life or your career, more than anything else in the world.

ABUNDANCE

Imagine you have all the resources, all the talent, all the money, any attribute you want. What would your dream be then? Who will you see? Talk to? What will you eat? Where will you go?

FOCUS

Make a huge sign that declares your dream and place it in front of wherever you sleep so it's the first thing you see when you wake up in the morning.

MAP

Identify at least three people who already live your dream. Research their stories of how they came to be where they are now.

APPROACH

Write down the steps and turning points along the way for at least two of the people who are already living your dream. Check in with yourself. Did you make any discoveries? Any surprises? Did these exercises change how you feel about your dream? Do you still want the same dream? Make adjustments if things change until you find the right fit.

VISION

Cut out words and images from magazines, postcards, posters, or anything that is inspiring for your dream. Add them to the area where your huge sign is/would be. Add more any time you find more you wish to add.

ACCOMPLISHMENT

Write down your accomplishments, near-missed accomplishments, any time anyone said or did anything that was affirming to your dream, even opportunities that you did not act on.

PLAN

Write down the steps of what you feel needs to happen for you to live your dream. First try starting with where you are now and go forward. Next, start with living your dream now and work backwards to how you came to be there. Only write down what you imagine will be needed, don't worry if it's complete or accurate.

INVENTORY

List your strengths and then list any areas that need strengthening.

PIECES

Now make a master list, taking in everything you've done so far and list all the things that need to change or occur between where you are now and when you are living your dream. Don't worry about the order, just one list with everything you know right now.

IMPACT

Now, put the items on your master list in the order of impact. Start with what would make the biggest difference to move you closer to your dream right now. Then work your way down to what would have the smallest impact on your dream. Label these from A-Z.

ENERGY

Make a second master list, this time starting with what would be the easiest and fastest thing to do on your master list down to what would be the most challenging. Label these from 1-100.

BALANCE

Fill out two columns (a letter column and a number column) side by side, with each item in order from top to bottom.Allocate time in your week to work on your dream. It could be 30 minutes or an hour at 10 am each day. Whatever time you decide to give to your dream, spend 80% of that time working on the top item of your A-Z list the very first thing when you start to work, then the 20% of the time that's left, work on the top of the list starting with 1-100.

SUPPORT

Who in your life supports your dream? Who believes you will do it? Who enjoys listening to you share your ideas, feelings, experiences?

EROSION

Who in your life is a skeptic or a critic? Who tells you that you or your dreams are unrealistic? Or that this will only lead to disappointment? Or a waste of time? Or that it will never pay the rent?

COMMUNITY

Who are the five people you spend the most time with? Do you believe that the more time you spend with people who believe in you, the more likely you are to live the life you were meant to live?

DISCRIMINATION

If any of the 5 people you spend the most time with is a negative influence, could you spend less time with them? If that is not something you are ready to do, could you at least protect your dream by never discussing it with them?

PERSPECTIVE

Remind yourself when you are with anyone who does not support your dream, that their criticism is defining who they are, NOT your dreams, or who you are or what you are here on this planet to do. Only you know your purpose.

NURTURE

Surround yourself with things that make you feel well cared for, that make you feel good, that you would still want to have around you in your dream life. Throw away or give away anything that does not have all those qualities.

GRATITUDE

Before you get out of bed each day and before you go to sleep, say one new thing for which you are grateful.

SENSES

Spend 5 minutes each day this week treating yourself to something that nourishes a different one of your senses.

DETAIL

Spend 5 minutes each day for a week sitting in the same place, somewhere in nature that you love and observe new things each day.

LAUGHTER

Spend 5 minutes each day this week watching something that you find laugh-out-loud-funny.

GOLDEN HOUR

MORNING ROUTINE: Experiment with a morning routine. Begin one day with a large glass of water first thing before any other beverages or food or cell phone or tv or email. Go for a walk or do some kind of exercise you like. Then have a nourishing breakfast. I like a green smoothie. What is the healthiest breakfast you can imagine trying? What we eat first in the day will set in motion what our body will desire that day. Try other things if you want to add them: Meditate? Journal? Stretching? Gratitude? Prayer? Affirmations? The focus is on making your body stronger.

PREPARATION

EVENING ROUTINE: what can you do tonight to make tomorrow more fulfilling? Write out what you want to accomplish tomorrow? Prioritize it by what will make the biggest difference in your life and make that the very first thing you tackle in your day? Set out your clothes and anything you need to do for the day? Meditate? Journal? Read? Brush your teeth? Shower? Beauty routine? Make tomorrow's lunch? The focus is on whatever you can do tonight that will make your day smoother, more relaxing, or more enjoyable tomorrow.

STRENGTH

How is your health? Are there any things you would like to be different? What could they be? What's a little thing you could do each day? Even for 1 minute? How would you like to strengthen your body?

MOVEMENT

Do you exercise? Do you enjoy exercising? Is there any sort of exercise that you might enjoy more? Would you like to try that? How could you make that happen even on the smallest scale?

MEDITATION

Meditation happens in so many forms. Do you have a meditation practice?

SLEEP

Sleep hygiene is primary. Is the room completely dark? Do you wear an eye mask? How much time before bed elapses before you sleep? Have you tried ear plugs? Do you LOVE your bed? Your pillows? Your bedding? You spend a third of your life here. It is your greatest opportunity to restore your vitality. Treat yourself to the best.

WATER

Water quality and quantity. We are mostly water. How much do you drink a day? Only water counts for 'drinking water'. Is your water excellent quality and free from harmful chemicals? Treat yourself to the best.

CREATIVITY

Creativity is as essential to well being as sleep, food, air, home and water. Creativity is a way of approaching something. Do you treat yourself to a practice of creative activities you love?

AWAKEN

Each of my five senses are intoxicated by...?

PLAY

How do you like to play? When did you try something new? Do you play every day?

NATURE

Spending time in nature is rejuvenating and reminds us of who we really are. Do you have a nature spot you like to go to? Do you like to walk? How does nature inspire you?

FREEDOM

Unclutter a space and you will unclutter a stuck area in your life.

FLOW

Organize a space and you will bring good change and flow to an area that is stagnant.

INTENTION

Make a plan to do a thing that energizes you when you think about doing it.

SKILLS

Take inventory of your skills. How many of them do you love to do? Are there skills you would love to master?

RESPONSIBILITY

Accept full responsibility for everything in your life. How does that feel?

COMMITMENT

What would need to change to have every person, place, and thing in your life designed to support your dream?

COMPLETION

Completion of the incomplete is a catalyst for change. What is incomplete in your life?

DECIDE

Make a new decision, large or small, right now. One that brings you relief, joy, excitement or some good feeling. You deserve to feel good..

PRIORITY

Commit to your top priority. Take action now towards your top priority.

BEGIN

Start a daily practice of some sort to move you towards your dream.

FOUNDATION

Foundation = home, money, growth, support How is your foundation? Does it fortify your life?

ROUTINE

Daily routines - am/pm, skills, industry, mindset How are your daily routines? Do they support your growth?

TIME

Some strategies to save time could be...?

COLLABORATE

Target your dream collaborators. Who are they? Send them an invitation.

INITIATE

Produce your own...?

RECEIVE

Receive the support of a coach. Who would be a great coach for you and your dream?

EXPLORE

Take a class or workshop with someone you admire.

IDENTIFY

Social media is my...

INVENT

MIND

Mindset is our infinite power source to create our life. Are you using this super power of yours to create?

INTUITION

Intuition + practice = luck

How lucky are you?

TRUST

Self-trust. Do you trust yourself?
How could you trust yourself more?

CARE

Self-care. How would you like to take better care of yourself?

HAPPINESS

What gives you a visceral sense of pleasure?

CHALLENGE

What challenges you, engages you to the point of losing track of time?

MEANING

What gives you a sense of meaningfulness to life?

FUN

What gives you both pleasure and challenges you?

VALUE

What gives you both pleasure and meaning?

PURPOSE

What gives you both meaning and challenges you?

JOY

What gives you all three: pleasure, challenge and meaning?

BELONG

What in your life makes you feel that life is worth living?

CLUES

I started out thinking I was writing a step-by-step book about how to help actors get to their ‘next level’.

But do we really need another step-by-step-to-success book? There are already so SO many of those voices— in blog posts and books and you tube videos and social media posts and conversations and schools and kitchens and boardrooms. They are everywhere. Countless versions of the outside-in approach. A one size fits all idea of where we should be. Always telling us we need to be somewhere other than where we are now. Teaching us to aspire to someone’s idea of what it means to succeed.

I am not saying it is a bad way to accomplish tangible goals. But does it *work*?

What if that way doesn’t resonate with you? What if that road gives you a sinking feeling? The feeling that there is an inescapable widening in the gap between self and oneself? A feeling like you are slowly (or not so slowly) falling through the cracks of life? Or what if you tried it, thinking it would change everything, but it didn’t? And you feel even worse and more hopeless?

There is another way. An inside-out approach. The one that allows the full bloom of joy to take root, to sprout, to grow, and grow stronger, to blossom, to bear the original fruit of its glory then fall to the earth where its seeds will land on new ground and begin again.

What makes you feel good? When do you perk up? When do you lean in? When do you feel alive, so engaged that time has flown but you are still still? Just busy being here and now? What are you doing in the moment you remember how precious life is? Where are you called to serve?

Listen

Respond

Pursue

Invest

Serve

JOY

www.ingramcontent.com/pod-product-compliance
Lightning Source LLC
LaVergne TN
LVHW052050160826
845678LV00015B/3153

* 9 7 9 8 8 4 8 1 5 4 3 9 9 *